Plus 1, Minus 1

Ann H. Matzke

ROURKE PUBLISHING
www.rourkepublishing.com

www.rourkepublishing.com

PHOTO CREDITS: Cover: © billyfoto, © Bloodua; Title Page: © kilukilu; Page 3: © Brent Hathaway; Page 4, 5, 6: © Liliboas; Page 7: © cgering; Page 8, 9, 10, 11: © Les Cunliffe; Page 11: © Anatoliy Samara; Page 12, 14: © GlobalP, © syagci; © HannamariaH; Page 13: © GlobalP; Page 15: © Barbara Helgason; Page 16, 17, 18: © burwellphotography; Page 19: © jcphoto; Page 20, 21, 22: © carlosalvarez; Page 23: © Craig Lopetz

Edited by Kelli L. Hicks

Cover and Interior design by Tara Raymo

Library of Congress Cataloging-in-Publication Data

Matzke, Ann H.
 Plus 1, minus 1 / Ann H. Matzke.
   p. cm. -- (Little world math concepts)
 Includes bibliographical references and index.
 ISBN 978-1-61590-294-1 (Hard Cover) (alk. paper)
 ISBN 978-1-61590-533-1 (Soft Cover)
 1. Mathematical notation--Juvenile literature. 2. Mathematical notation. I. Title.
 QA41.M37 2011
 513.2'11--dc22
                        2010009280

Rourke Publishing
Printed in the United States of America, North Mankato, Minnesota
033010
033010LP

www.rourkepublishing.com - rourke@rourkepublishing.com
Post Office Box 643328 Vero Beach, Florida 32964

Plus one adds one. Minus one takes one away.

Let's count and see.

Pick four flowers.

$4 + 1 = ?$

Pick one more.

1

2

3

4

5

Now count the flowers.

Five flowers smell so sweet.

Four colorful markers.

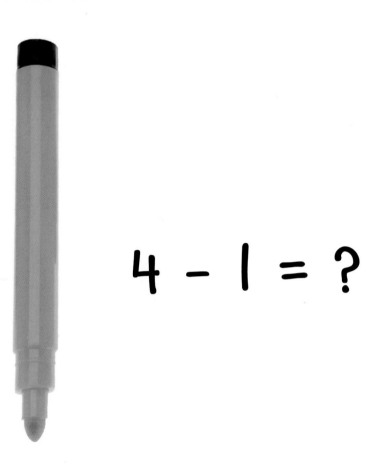

$$4 - 1 = ?$$

Give one away.

1   2   3

Now count the markers.

Three colorful markers.

Five puppies play.

$$5 + 1 = ?$$

Plus one more.

1

2

3

4 5 6

Now count the puppies.

Six playful puppies.

Bake five cookies.

$$5 - 1 = \text{?}$$

Take one away.

1

2

3

4

Now count the cookies.

Four cookies. Yum. Yum!

Three bikes stopped.

$$3 + 1 = ?$$

Add one more.

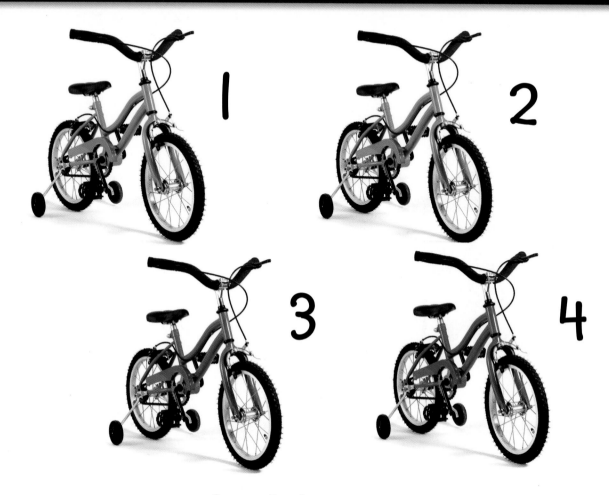

1

2

3

4

Now count the bikes.

Four bikes ready to ride!

23

Index

Websites

www.ixl.com/math/grade/kindergarten/

www.ixl.com/math/practice/grade-1-subtracting-1

www.kidsnumbers.com/sunny-bunny-subtraction.php

About the Author

Ann Matzke is an elementary library integration specialist at an elementary school in Gothenburg, Nebraska. Every day at least one book is checked out and one book is checked in at her library. Ann lives in Gothenburg, Nebraska near an original Pony Express Station and enjoys reading and writing.